FROM THE YOUNG

An "inadequate" perspective

From the Young

an "inadequate" perspective

Copyright © 2019 by A. A. Miller

Edited by Gabbie Cavett

First Edition

Writings by A. A. Miller unless indicated otherwise. All quotes are public domain

ISBN: 978-1-689-45989-1

Independently published

To Elliott P. Orr,
your inheritance of
love and memories
will last forever.

Table of Contents

Preface

"So many people live within unhappy
circumstances and yet will not take
the initiative to change their situation
because they are conditioned to a life
of security, conformity, and conservatism,
all of which may appear to give one peace
of mind, but in reality nothing is more
damaging to the adventurous spirit
within a man than a secure future.
The very basic core of a man's living
spirit is his passion for adventure.
The joy in life comes from our encounters
with new experiences and hence there is
no greater joy than to have an endlessly
changing horizon, for each day to have
a new and different sun."

— Christopher McCandless

Introduction

Dear Humanity,

Inside this letter you will find writings, thoughts, quotes, and questions about human life and our interpersonal connections.

Life is a continuous process of change. *From the Young* is a collection of writings centered around society and how humans operate in it. It opens a conversation to challenge the way people think about things in life and why some things are deliberately overlooked in communities and nations. It is not a book of answers—merely passages to provoke thought and encourage time of reflection.

Apathy is no longer an acceptable excuse for ignorance, cognitive dissonance, or indifference itself. No generation has been perfect; however, in a new generation that is growing faster than anyone can comprehend, it is time for discussion on topics that are being ignored. *From the Young* is a starting place for those with open minds.

KNOWLEDGE

―――

"Knowledge itself is power."

— Sir Francis Bacon

Knowledge is power,

Knowledge is everything,

Knowledge is life,

Knowledge is where everything begins.

Spend less time fearing the unknown and start discovering it.

Cliche thoughts are the most dangerous thoughts of all.

Profound statements mean nothing.

False statements are accepted as truth.

"You may delay, but time will not."

— Benjamin Franklin

If you write your own rules,

you can never lose.

"*Another one of the old poets, whose name has escaped my memory at present, called Truth the daughter of Time.*"

— Aulus Gellius

Knowledge is a collection of facts and information acquired through time and experiences.

The implementation of knowledge

Is conversation

Is wisdom

Is advice

Is joyful

Is sadness

Is what continues the human race.

Knowledge is wisdom or knowledge is folly.

Knowledge comes before wisdom.

There are denotations of words.

There are connotations of words.

"It is a capital mistake to theorize before one has data. Insensibly one begins to twist facts to suit theories, instead of theories to suit facts."

— Sherlock Holmes, *A Study in Scarlet,* Sir Arthur Conan Doyle

People perceive things based off of what they know or assume to know.

If they come to you in public,

you have permission to respond in public.

If they come to you in private,

you respond in private.

Why is greater than what.

There's a lot of wisdom in knowing how to just be.

From the Young

SOCIETY

—

"In the country of the blind,
the one-eyed man is king."

— Erasmus

We live in society,

not under its reign.

Popular opinion drives society.
Popular opinion often supersedes truth.
Society tells us to conform.
With popular opinion comes Majority
and her rules. Objection to any
minute detail within her beliefs
is an immediate banishment to
the Island of Leper, for outcasts.

"Wrong does not cease to be wrong because the majority share in it."

— Leo Tolstoy

Sometimes, we focus so much on Bad

that Good becomes a stranger.

Don't strive to blend in with society. Average is a disease.

Average wants a safe destination—even in death.

Destiny demands extrodinary. Eradicate normal.

The best thing to carry with you is confidence.

The internet will still exist tomorrow. What is the rush?

I knew a man who never used the internet…

and lived.

"Wise men speak because they have something to say; fools because they have to say something."

— Plato

Your response in public is your intake in private.

We can't blame situations on heritage.

We have choices to make in the present.

All we know is war and the struggle for power.

Is war equated with peace?

All we know is debt to our debtors.

Is slavery the real freedom?

All we know is what we need for our personal existence.

Is ignorance stronger than knowledge?

Let us stop stripping away our children's innocence.

Words we should use less:

If

Fine

Good

Perfect

Always

Never

Social media shows us a false way to live.

Yet, we are drawn to that way of life, that way of acceptance,

that way of communication, that way of love.

Social media isn't social.

Stop sharing your feelings on social media. If you do, know that others will as well. You have no right to get offended about someone's opinion right under your own.

I have allowed too many voices inside my head.

It's hard to make a peaceful decision.

If the entire world deleted social media for a day. . .

We are a grain of sand trying to explain the ocean.

Social media doesn't care about your feelings.

Silence is the absence of social media.

"The world is full of obvious things which nobody by any chance ever observes."

– Sherlock Holmes, *The Hound of the Baskervilles*,
Sir Arthur Conan Doyle

Logical fallacies are used everyday for the benefit of oneself.

From the Young

LOVE

"Being deeply loved by someone gives you strength,
while being loved deeply gives you strength."

— Lao Tzu

Time: beginning, middle, end. Measuring how long something
has existed.

In order for love to be love, it must exist outside of time,
otherwise it is malleable, shifting like the ways of the winds
or someone's thoughts.

Space: the physical space that we take up. The air around you
and the distance it takes to get there.

In order for love to be love, it must exist outside of space,
otherwise it is confined to the space you allow it to occupy
In your mind.

Reason: the logic we create to comprehend concepts.

In order for love to be love, it must exist outside of human
reasoning, otherwise it is limited to our personal reasoning
and has a different depth to each person. No wonder sometimes
it doesn't correlate between people or communities.
We are taking something in part when it was never designed
to be used in pieces. If you don't have it all there to start,
it isn't true.

Love exists outside of space, time, and reason.

Love

Love is not a variable. There is nothing that needs to be added to love to make it significant. It's not, "I love you times infinity." There is no measurement of love. "I love you to the moon and back" is actually an insult to whom you are referring, putting a limit on how far you would go for someone. But then, isn't that the point? How far we would go no matter the odds? You see, love is not just a verb. Love is a noun.

True love does not depend on outside forces. "If this, then that…" No. Love exists outside of time, space, and reason. It passes humans' comprehension. It is not limited to the bounds you and I are. If it was, it would also be human, changing like someone's feelings.

Love is constant. It is always present. Love should build you up, not tear you down.Love is patient. Love honors others.Love is kind. Love keeps no records of wrongs.Love is not self-seeking. Love is unconditional. Love lacks pride. Love is not jealous. Love is humble. Love is slow to anger.Love always protects, always trusts, always hopes, and always perseveres.

When you start to think as one.

When you build each other up.

When you support each other at all times.

When there is complete trust.

When you protect each other from battles.

When you throw away the scorecard.

When you find true joy and contentment.

When you aren't envious of others.

When you don't dishonor others.

When you seeking the desires of their heart.

When you build upon kindness, patience, peace, hope, and truth.

When you satisfy their needs before yours.

When you know your true worth and their worth.

When you would give anything for them.

It may risk your reputation, your convenience,

or success, but those shall be pale compared

to the saturated life of perfect inheritance--love,

memories, and a bond that will never be broken.

The theme of selflessness, sacrifice, loyalty, honor, truth, and respect are found within love. Without one, it cannot be considered love. Society tells us that we can love someone without being entirely loyal. Or, that love exists without the presence of selflessness and respect. These are lies. We (I, even) wonder why we can't find the right "one". Maybe it is because we, ourselves, aren't our true self as we get into relationships. Or, we are broken and seeking healing in a person who cannot–and should not–offer that.

Energy cannot be created or destroyed.

Love cannot be created or destroyed.

Emotions

Attraction

Infatuation

Lust

Can be created and destroyed.

Our thoughts and feelings can align with love.

To say they are inseparable or codependent is false.

A conditional aspect of love is obligatory reciprocity.

That is not love. That is an accord agreed upon beforehand or demanded afterward.

Fluency in love is far greater than any language.

Love is a universal language.

Sonnet 116

– William Shakespeare

Your significant other should not make you who you are.

I always believed a relationship could heal me. I've never been so wrong when it comes to the foundation of what love exists for. Mended hearts are found within and through love, but not the beginning. Healing is not the goal when forming intimate relationships. If it becomes the foundation, you will start to see cracks as time goes on.

If things are never brought to light,

they will reveal themselves when they have doubled in size.

We hold our hearts back in relationships because we've all seen a bad relationship end.

When I'm with you, the world means nothing.

For the world has its way, but mine is you.

True love is manipulation free.

Pornography destroys the individual.

Pornography destroys the family.

Pornography destroys the community.

Pornography hurts my community.

Pornography hurts my family.

Pornography hurts me.

We guard the inner parts of our hearts, not allowing anyone to access them.

The full, raw version of love is scary. Maybe, subconsciously, we shy away from true definitions of words because changing our life's state is far too inconvenient for us to follow through with it.

Will we ever be able to comprehend love to its fullest extent?

It's the unforeseen.

It's the unexpected.

It's the undeserving.

From the Young

COMPARISON

"Comparison is the thief of joy."

— Theodore Roosevelt

We will never win comparing two things. When we compare ourselves to others, we will always find at least one thing in the other person's life that makes us feel lesser. And, on the rare chance we happen to be "better" than them, we still lose because we have insulted their appearance, character, or integrity. Whether or not we believe to be better than them, one or both sides have been affected by this unnecessary, uncalled for evaluation. No one asked for this examination except the insecurities of our heart.

Negativity is so prevalent in society becasue we have created too many "languages" for describing flaws in ourselves and others.

If your self-esteem is based on what others think of you,
it isn't self-esteem. Don't allow others to decide how you are
going to feel about yourself.

We feel insecure when we compare ourselves in unfair situations.

We compare our beginnings to other's completions.

Comparison is soon followed by

Anxiety

Depression

Stress

Discouragement

Misery

Despair

Desolation

No one has a right to judge others. We are all imperfect.

From the Young

APPEARANCE

"Infatuation craves perfection."

— Madeline Roy

Modern media,

marketing schemes,

masterpieces and

multitudes

mislead us:

"You are worthy

once you have

achieved a

certain look,

status or level."

Beauty is physical

Beauty is not physical

Beauty is visual

Beauty is not visual

Beauty is symmetrical

Beauty is not symmetrical

Beauty is found in all

Do not live in the illusion that someone is perfect

or the delusion that you are.

Everyone fights for the spotlight on their good

yet stop at nothing to move the light off their bad.

It is impossible to perform on and off stage simultaneously.

UNWORTHINESS

"Failure does not equate to unworthiness."

— John C. Grey

Maybe

We

Feel

Unworthy

Because

We

Seek

Affirmation

In

The

Wrong

Places

Your past does not define you.

You are not a failure because you have problems.

You are not a failure because of those who've wronged you.

Unworthiness

Misery loves company…

Criticism is envious of love's power.

Unworthiness comes from our own interpretation of our actions based on the assumption of other's perceptions or perspective.

You can't depend on anyone to make you feel a certain way.

You are untouchable if you victimize yourself. You are seeking healing; however, you cannot achieve that if you distance yourself from those who love you.

No one can show you your true worth

until you know your true worth.

If I don't show my weakness, they won't know I'm not capable.

From the Young

CONFIDENCE

"You gain strength, courage, and confidence
by every experience in which you really stop
to look fear in the face. You are able to say
to yourself, 'I lived through this horror.
I can take the next thing that comes along.'"

— Eleanor Roosevelt

Confidence is a mental battle.

The voice inside my head isreplaced by the voices of my tormentors. It is hard to keep track of both sides. Some days, I can't tell the difference.

We can choose to fight Fear and its allies—anxiety, depression, unworthiness, hate—or choose to be imprisoned by the inability to let go of our past.

Fear of embarrassment,

Fear of speaking,

Fear of thinking,

Fear of making the wrong decision.

Who said the only way to live is to surround yourself with fear?

If fear is the foundation of our actions and decisions, we will become the opposite of what we wish to be.

A foundation of fear is step one to failure.

A foundation of fear isn't living at all.

Stop fearing the unknown and start discovering it.

Never step outside of your comfort zone. Taking a step outside implies retreating at the end of the moment, day, week, month, year. Congratulations. You are right where you started.

Your mindset should be to expand your comfort zone, adding to what you are comfortable with. . .permanently.

The hardest thing we have to do is address our pain rather than allowing it to sit in the back of our mind–festering into something we don't want it to be.

Confidence is not found in social media, likes, or followers.

Life is not measured by the number of followers you receive.

INTENTIONALITY

---

*"Human nature is evil, and goodness
is caused by intentional activity."*

— Xun Kuang

Life without intention isn't life at all.

It is easy to focus on the negative. You don't have to look far to find it. Be intentional with finding hope in your life.

Go with all your heart.

Intentions show where your heart is.

Asking for help is hard but rewarding.

Be careful when you use the word perfect.

I want to be intentional with the relationships I have and the way I operate within them.

AUTHENTICITY

"Don't trade your authenticity for approval."

— Anonymous

It is hardly ever about what you do but your heart that is behind it.

The greatest trick I have ever learned is how to hide my apathy with counterfeit authenticity.

Be proud of whatever you put your name on.

We live in a conflicting world. People seek approval from those outside of their personalities in exchange for confidence. Contrary, the newest generation is all about being authentic, proving to others what life should be.

Which is it?

Being true to yourself or compromising your character, honor, integrity, and language to have a stamp of approval from society?

From the Young

COMMUNICATION

"Communication is essential in relationships."

— Richard J.

If, at any point, anger joins one or more parties in how they communicate, a conflict will never be resolved until anger leaves.

It is hard to show sincerity through a screen.

We assume things, interpret things, and communicate things
at the wrong time, place, tone, context.
Now, throw in a screen…

The internet connects us.

The internet does not communicate for us.

This is how enemies are made:

miscommunication and misinterpretation.

"~~I'm fine.~~"

Problems with communication arise without
Listening's presence.

Your heart and mind are separate. When aligned, your beliefs and thoughts are communicated clearly. When disconnected, contradiction enters.

From the Young

FRIENDSHIP

———

*"I don't need a friend who changes when I change
and who nods when I nod; my shadow does
that much better."*

— Plutarch

True	Friendship
Is	Perfectly
Balanced	In
Effort	Time
Happiness	Sadness
Easy	Hard

Friendship must be built on solid foundations.

Collecting the title of friendship when times are good is one of the easiest tasks. Staying true to that title when things are not going as planned is essential in a true relationship.

If they were there for you once,

they will be there for you again…

you just have to ask.

True friends are hard to come by.

Our definition of friend is far from the truth. A friend is not someone you only interact with through the internet and social media. A friend is not someone who puts zero effort into building your relationship, regardless of long you have known them. A friend is not someone who smiles to your face while stabbing you in the back. A friend is true, honorable, and noble through everything.

My loneliness is self-inflicted

because I don't let anyone in.

From the Young

FORGIVENESS

"A grudge is a heavy thing to carry."

— Unknown

Forgiveness isn't common in the world

and it can be shocking when it happens.

Unforgiveness is drinking poison and hoping the other person dies.

Without forgiveness, you will never be free.

You have forgiven them when you:

        Resist thoughts of revenge

        Don't seek to do them mischief

        Wish them well

        Grieve at their calamities

        Seek reconciliation

        Are always willing to come to their aid

Forgiveness is not:

    Approval of what they did

    Denying what they did

    Excusing what they did

    Refusing to take it seriously

    Justifying what they did

    Pretending you aren't hurt

    Keeping score

    Using your power to make them pay

    Elevating yourself

    Taking offense easily

Reconciliation is different than forgiveness.

I am crippled by the unforgiveness in my heart.

Sorry can be a manipulative tool.

Sorry without change is a lie.

LOYALTY

"Those who don't know the value of loyalty
can never appreciate the cost of betrayal."

— Anonymous

Emotions, feelings, and thoughts play a role on the strength of loyalty.

Values and beliefs create brotherhoods and enemies.

Loyalty leads to trust.

COMMITMENT

"..."

— Anonymous

Let us take a step back.

At times, it's not even about remaining loyal. We don't even commit in the first place. We struggle with allowing ourselves to commit to anything. As soon as someone or something gets close in our lives, we want to push it out. Letting it in could lead to the result of us getting hurt…again. Our scars are so deep within us. Even a small scratch can create a new scar.

Commitment is being devoted to a cause, a belief, or obligation that restricts freedom. It is pledging yourself to something greater.

Words and actions show where a person's allegiance resides.

RESPECT

———

"Respect yourself and others will respect you."

— Confucius

You cannot give what you do not have.

Human logic:

"I don't have an apple, therefore,
I cannot give an apple to you."

"I don't have love, joy, wisdom,
however, let me give it to you."

This fundamental value is overlooked everyday. Respect is not giving someone a substitute to the real thing.

Respect's existence is not conditional. If you do this for me, I will return the favor or gift. Within conditional agreements, many original aspects are lost to space and time, such as the respect you want from others. You are no longer an honorable individual, but an excellent barginer. Love and selflessness are removed from the equation, resulting in a legal issue that usually takes years to sort out. Mathematicians and scientists alike are baffled by the complexity of the equation. It wasn't supposed to be like that in the first place. Maybe it cannot be measured because there is more than one variable. I am okay with some things being just out of reach of human comprehension.

From the Young

HOPE

"Where there's life, there's hope."

— Theocritus

Fear is contagious.

Hope is contagious.

"Choose to see the good."

— Elliott P. Orr

You do not have to look far to see the darkness within the world. It is all around you. The abundance of darkness makes it easy to focus on negativity.

Find something that brings you peace in a world full of chaos.

There is a difference between hope and positivity. Positivity ignores the bad. Hope sees both the good and the bad and chooses the good despite any circumstance.

What does life look like without hope?

Is there even a desire to live?

Your perspective, your beliefs, and your values all play a factor in what hope you have.

RELIGION

—

"Science without religion is lame,
religion without science is blind."

— Albert Einstein

Religion is such a sensitive subject.

Religion is a specific system of faith and worship.

Faith is complete trust in someone or something.

Worship is an expression of reverence.

Everything you say,

Everything you do,

Everything you love,

Everything you hate,

Is your religion.

People are passionate about what they believe.

We all live by different beliefs.

Let's not blame things on heritage.

Each time we compare an imperfect thing (us) to something we know or hold to be perfect, it will always result in confusion, contradiction, and skewed communication.

If no one is perfect, doesn't this include behaviors even under their religion?

POLITICS

—

"Always vote for principle, though you may vote alone, and you may cherish the sweetest reflection that your vote is never lost."

— John Quincy Adams

"War is not an independent phenomenon, but the continuation of politics by different means."

— Carl von Clausewitz

Good versus evil is in the heart, not in politics, morality, or legality.

Anger

Rage

Hatred

Fury

Jealousy

Resentment

Pride

Prejudice

Get you nowhere in conversations, discussions, and debates.

You can never win an argument. There are two sides. If you lose, you have lost. If you win, you have still lost. By winning, you have weakened, destroyed, or changed their spirits or beliefs. Did you truly win? Pride says yes. Proving your point across is not always winning. Beliefs, values, and thoughts should not be treated this way. Even if you end up being right, you may lose rapport with your opponent.

Anger is a good reaction

but a terrible solution.

PEACE

"Those who are free of resentful
thoughts surely find peace."

— Buddha

Thoughts that fill your head keep you from a peace-filled life.

The unseen prison is your mind.

Don't think about penguins. If you want something to change, you have to replace it with something entirely new. If you want to stop the penguins, start thinking about giraffes. If you want anxiety out of you life, you can't think about anxiety. To replace something, another thing must take its place; otherwise, you will be left with a void that can only be filled by the thing you just "threw away." If you focus your thoughts and life with the bad, it will consume you until there is nothing left to think about. With one thousand thoughts running through your mind, how can you find peace?

Peace is different than security.

Peace is freedom of fear.

Security is the coexistence of fear.

Security has room for fear,

yet you feel well enough protected to go on.

A life free of fear is a life of peace.

Clarity comes when we quiet the noise.

Listening is a virtue that can offer peace.

"Your anxiety is lying to you."

– Unknown

Follow peace.

When it comes to decision making, you will make the right choice when you have peace with both sides.

I find myself having therapy sessions with those I trust.

"*Five great enemies to peace inhabit with us: avarice, ambition, envy, anger, and pride. If those enemies were to be banished, we should infallibly enjoy perpetual peace.*"

— Francesco Petrarch

Peace

Don't schedule peace
For the end of your day,
For the end of your week,
For the end of your year,
For the end of your life.

From the Young

UNITY

"In union there is strength."

— Aesop

Unity is much more than just being in close proximity to someone.

Division is the longest lasting war.

Division among brothers,

Division of beliefs,

Division of cultures,

Division.

Lack of unity is the earliest sign of destruction within kingdoms, relationships, and communities.

The absence of unity or the attempt to form unity is an answer that covers a lot of questions we ask.

Lies we believe:

No one relates to me.

No one will understand.

I am alone.

Two can accomplish more than twice as much as one.

Move at the speed of unity.

Tough vs. Critical

Unity can be a common vision.

Unity can be a common enemy.

KINDNESS

"That best portion of a good man's life,

his little, nameless, unremembered acts

of kindness and of love."

— William Wordsworth

If you remember a stranger's name you have passed the first step of a relationship.

Acknowledging people when you are out and about will serve you and others greatly.

If your community exists to serve you, you have relationships for the wrong reasons. If your community exists and you are the only one serving—giving your gifts, talents, and time—you have a good start, but not all of it. In a true relationship, no one should ask themselves, "What might I get out of this?" Rather, "What can I do for this person?" If everyone focused on that, I wonder what our communities would look like.

Do not mistake my kindness for weakness.

Using kindness for personal gain isn't kindness.

JOY

———

"When you do things from your soul,
you feel a river moving in you, a joy."

— Rumi

Joy is not something we retire to in life.

Joy

We live our whole lives struggling with happiness only to retire with joy and peace. Where was it the past sixty years?

Sometimes we spend so much time trying to provide for our families that we forget to provide for our families.

.

We sacrifice so much to get what we desire that we forget to go after joy.

They say money can't buy happiness. It can.

What are you really searching for? Joy.

Nothing can buy that.

Joy

Joy can come easier depending on your surroundings. If you choose to live in a hopeless mindset, it might not be that it isn't there; you choose not to notice it and live in it.

Happiness is temporary, like the objects you posses.

Joy is eternal, like the qualities we carry with us.

People place their happiness in materials, living in the moment,

not knowing when it will be stripped away from them.

If there is someone in your life who constantly drags you down—won't allow you to be happy or will not celebrate your victories—consider living your life without them in it. Most of the time it is us choosing to drag on the continuation of our misery. We have a choice. You can choose the people in your life. You can choose who you give access to your heart. You can stop at any point. You never signed a legal agreement with your friend from grade school. You have the power to surround yourself with those who want to build you up. You can choose joy.

If your life is based on the foundation of a hurt that has never healed, you will not find joy in that state. Joy comes from a healed heart, soul, and mind. Complacency and laziness will never get you to a new location.

Joy is always on the other side of the right decision.

HONOR

—

"I would prefer even to fail with
honor than win by cheating."

— Sophocles

Honor is only honor if the person you are honoring feels honored.

Honor is covered by the shadows of our selfish desires.

Honor is at war with deception, disloyalty, and disobedience.

INFLUENCE

"We convince by our presence."

— Walt Whitman

You have more reach, more influence on those around you if you are honest and genuine about your thoughts, actions, and words.

Misconceptions, assumptions, and lack of knowledge will forever be roadblocks when trying to reach the hearts of people.

Influence is having an effect on the character, development, or behavior of someone.

LEADERSHIP

―

"He who had never learned to obey
cannot be a good commander."

— Aristotle

Great leaders inspire greatness in others.

Serving shows your ability to lead.

Sometimes, the most obvious things still need to be said.

Failure is an investment into your future.

Authority is influence, not just a power.

We are scared to be leaders. True leadership usually lies in the land of the outsiders.

Obedience is better than efficiency.

Never hold back because others are holding back.

DISCOURAGEMENT

"My great concern is not whether you have failed,

but whether you are content with your failure."

— Abraham Lincoln

I refuse to let people identify me by my issues.

Identity does not come from peers, society, media, parents, etc…

Do you live in your biography

or your autobiography?

Discouragement

Rain seems endless going from a single drop to the next.

Timing is everything.

Timing is nothing.

Empathy, in its truest form, is a step in helping the discouraged.

The battlefield within the mind is the most dangerous one known to man.

I do the things I don't want to do

and I don't do the things I want to do.

Discouragement is a loss of confidence.

PERSPECTIVE

—

"I cannot teach anybody anything.
I can only make them think."

— Socrates

"Fear is only as deep as the mind allows."

— Japanese Proverb

If the goal of life is to arrive safely at death, what is the point?

"Say not always what you know, but always know what you say."

— Claudius

Detach yourself from the outcome
and attach yourself to the process.

You recieve the love you think you deserve.

We decide where the wilderness starts and where it ends.

Keep your friends close and your enemies closer,

for your enemies were once brothers.

There is a difference between positive feedback
and truthful feedback.

We have all been put in misery both friend and foe alike.

Not everyone acts the way you do or the way you want them to.

Even fools are thought to be wise if they keep silent.

"I hurt just as you do."

You will always be blindsided by the things you ignore.

Just because you are impatient doesn't mean the rules change.

Letdowns can be beautiful.

How can you have knowledge of what is good, right, light, positive when you live the very opposite way?

If we knew everything,
what would be the point?
If nothing bad happened,
would good exist?

We are all offenders.

You can't call it a sound judgement if you base it off of one thing, one person, one time, or one experience.

Appreciate what already is.

What you see depends on where you are standing.

It's looking back that makes you

glad you were brave enough to go.

Optimism vs. Pessimism

Change is always good.

There is a time for everything…

You can tell what someone truly thinks or believes by observing their words, actions, and normal routines when they face a crisis.

A road looks perfect from a distance

but up close is a different story.

Don't second guess yourself based on an outsider's perspective.

At times, it's best not to know all the inner workings of the organization you love.

*"I can control my passions and emotions
if I can understand their nature."*

– Spinoza

Sometimes,

It is not love,

Wisdom,

Advice,

Forgiveness,

Redemption,

Knowledge,

Authentic,

Kindness,

Honor,

Or inspiration;

It is just noise.

Did it lose its value and beauty,
or have you been familiarized to it?

I wouldn't change my times of misery and sorrow for more happy memories.

Not everyone acts the way you do
or the way that you want them to.

We all listen to something.

Speeches.

Voices.

Music.

Silence.

"My patience is wearing thin."
As if it is a gauge telling you
how much is left in the tank.

Should patience be something
you can measure or just something
that is present or absent like a switch?

If you stop expecting perfection in others
you won't be disappointed as easily.

Should moving on be something that happens in your heart or due to external forces?

There is more than one way to say something.

Often times, a different way is better.

*"It's not what you look at that matters,
it's what you see."*

— Henry David Thoreau

Deception can lie in the obvious. Guided misdirection.

Hiding in plain sight.

There are other perspectives outside your own.

The world is not defined by your likes and dislikes.

People are passionate when their life, reputation, or honor is on the line.

Learning never ends.

Evil appeals to the weak-hearted.

INSPIRATION

———

"Inspiration is propellant."

— Unknown

Inspiration in one's mind can start as a single dream, vision, goal, or thought that leads to another.

Inspiration is a timely idea.

There are people you will never be able to fully thank for what they did for you, directly or indirectly. Pay it forward.

Inspiration

Inspiration can be found in the midst of nothing.

Listen to those who inspire you and speak to those you inspire.

In order to turn on the lights, you must step into the dark room.

Everyone struggles with this: basing your decision off the past.

No.

Don't base your next decision off your past. You can study it in order to learn for the future, but you can't grow if you are trapped in previous mistakes. You have to be in the present to move forward.

Scientists say that bumblebees can't fly. They say they are too big with wings that are too small. Bees fly all the time; we know this. But imagine—for a moment—if they listened to the scientists and gave up before even trying. That, of course, was a statement they simply could not buy. You shouldn't listen to someone who tells you what you can and cannot do. Those people are insecure, jealous, or even hold anger towards you. They try to limit your aspirations by telling you what you can and cannot do. The moment you believe them, is the moment they have won. Be who you were made to be. Humble your critics. Those people are just sorry, sad scientists with statistics. Those scientists want to prove wrong any hypothesis that they deem not possible. The scientists spend too much time worrying about the bees in the room that they forget about the elephant–they are irresponsible. Because they aren't satisfied with their life, they feel their only choice is to see flaws in others. Now, why would you listen to someone who doesn't even have their life figured out? The bees who don't listen are the ones who go on to do great things whether or not the world knows about them. Deeds will not be less important because they go unmentioned. The bees are the ones who are alone together and together they stand alone. The bees are the ones who are being themselves while believing in themselves. So, just because someone thinks you can't fly, it doesn't mean they're right. The bees who don't listen have already taken flight.

From the Young

No matter how hard the task may get,

No matter if no one will follow you,

No matter if no one will listen to you,

No matter if something tries to stop you,

No matter if all lights go out,

No matter what your mind says,

Stay true to what your heart believes,

Even when you cannot see what is beyond.

LEGACY

———

"If I am in harmony with my family, that's success."

— Ute Proverb

Inheritance has nothing to do with monetary value.

It is the love and memories you shall cherish.

Your past is not your future.

Don't allow your present struggle

to supercede your past successes.

Regardless of whether the world knows your name at the time of your passing does not determine your legacy on Earth.

Your character, love, kindness, words, authenticity, deeds, knowledge, and responses are what will be left in the hearts you love and the hearts that love you.

Everyone wants to be remembered.

Let it be for the right reasons.

"A person often meets his destiny on the road he took to avoid it."

— Jean De La Fontaine

DREAMS

———

"Our imagination is paralyzed the day we limit our aspirations."

— A. A. Miller

Don't follow your dreams.

They aren't always what they seem.

Take your passions with you

and you'll find what you seek along the way.

Live with vision.

The only reason why your dream is out of reach is because you threw it away.

The reason why we walk around defeated is because we allow others to identify us by our issues or perceived issues. Once we believe them, we are locked into a prison within our minds.

You need to fight for every chance you want. You need to fight on behalf of your dreams. You don't have it already, so you have nothing to lose. Take each day one step at a time. Too often I see a friend, colleague, acquaintance, or stranger put a dream or hope on a shelf to collect dust.

"No one from my family has ever accomplished that."

"I'm just a kid from a town you've never heard of."

"I am too old to start something like that."

"No one has ever achieved something like this before."

"Twenty years from now you will be more disappointed by the things you didn't do than by the ones you did do. So throw off the bowlines. Sail away from the safe harbor. Catch the trade winds in your sails. Explore. Dream. Discover."

— Mark Twain

From,

The Young

Topics to explore in volume two:

Apathy

Anxiety

Isolation

Emotion

Zeal

67966413R00188